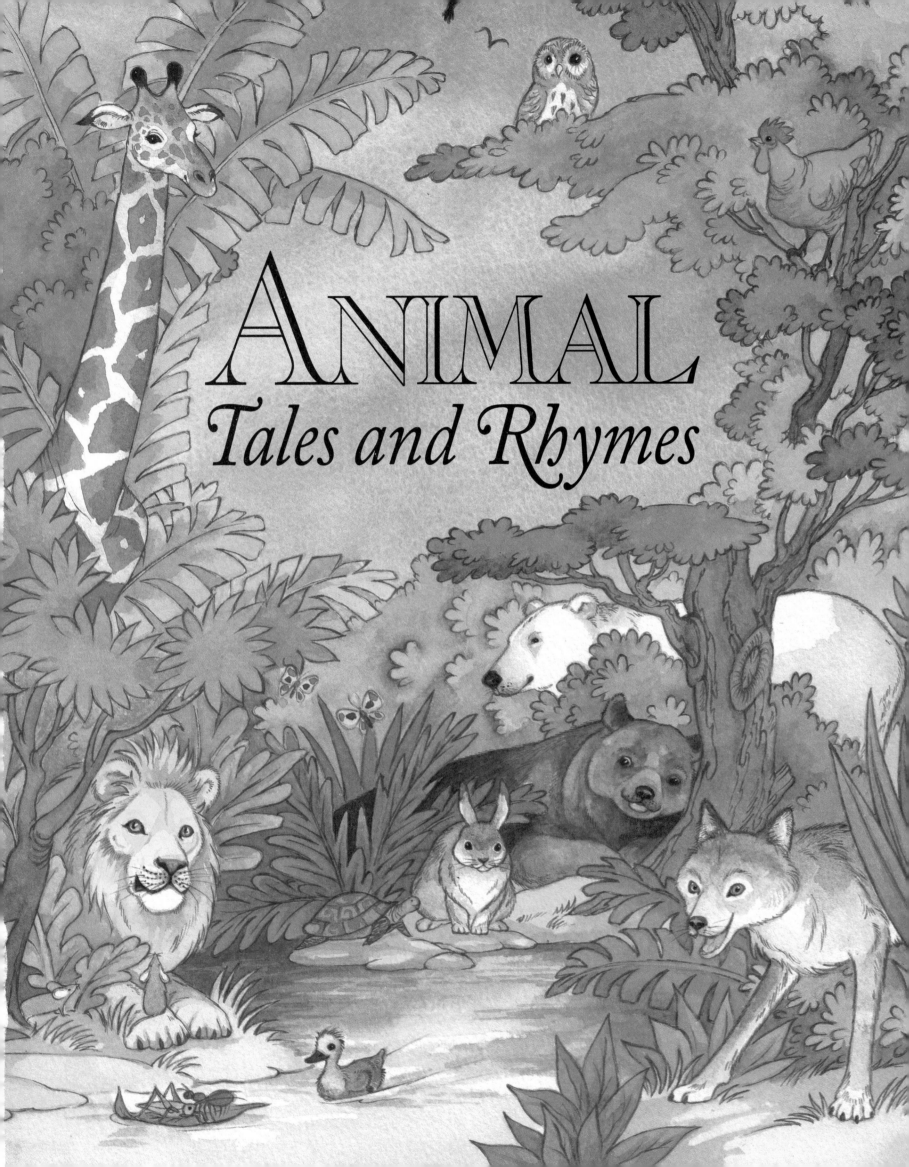

Animal
Tales and Rhymes

The Three Little Pigs

Once there were three little pigs who decided that the time had come for them to set off into the wide world and find homes of their own.

"Perhaps you are right, boys," said their mother. "But remember, watch out for the big, bad wolf!"

The little pigs kissed their mother and set off. Before long they became tired and sat down to rest. Just then a farmer went past, carrying a load of straw.

"With that straw I could build a strong, safe house," said the first little pig. "You two go on without me. I will stop right here."

So the first little pig said goodbye to his brothers and bought the load of straw from the farmer. He worked very hard and soon he had built the cutest little cottage you ever saw.

Meanwhile, the other two little pigs had walked a good deal further when they met a woodcutter carrying a load of sticks.

"With those sticks I could build a strong, safe house," said the second little pig. "You go on without me, brother. I will stop right here."

So the second little pig said goodbye to his brother and bought the load of sticks from the woodcutter. He worked even harder than the first little pig. By suppertime, he was standing outside the cutest little house you ever saw.

Meanwhile, the third little pig had walked even further. Late that afternoon, he met a workman with a cart piled high with fine building bricks.

"With those bricks I could build a strong, safe house," said the third little pig. "I will stop right here."

So the third little pig bought the cartload of bricks from the workman and he built the neatest little brick house you ever saw.

That night the first little pig slept soundly in his straw house. But at midnight there came a soft tapping on the door.

"Little pig, little pig, let me come in!" called a gruff voice.

It was the big, bad wolf! The first little pig shook with fright under the sheets but he answered bravely.

"No, no, by the hair of my chinny chin chin, I will not let you in!"

"Then I'll huff, and I'll puff, and I'll blow your house down!" shouted the wolf. And he huffed and he puffed and he blew with all his might. The house of straw blew down in a moment, but the first little pig ran as fast as he could to his brother's house of sticks.

The very next night the two little pigs were fast asleep in the house of sticks when there came a soft tapping on the door.

"Little pigs, little pigs, let me come in!" called a gruff voice.

You can guess who that was! The two little pigs trembled but they answered bravely.

"No, no, by the hair of our chinny chin chins, we will not let you in!"

"Then I'll huff, and I'll puff, and I'll blow your house down!" shouted the wolf. And he huffed and he puffed and he blew with all his might. The house of sticks blew down in a moment, but the two little pigs ran as fast as they could to their brother's house of bricks.

Another day passed and the three little pigs went to bed in the house of bricks. In the middle of the night there came a soft tapping on the door.

"Little pigs, little pigs, let me come in!" called a gruff voice.

The three little pigs knew at once who it was but they hugged each other and answered bravely.

"No, no, by the hair of our chinny chin chins, we will not let you in!"

"Then I'll huff, and I'll puff, and I'll blow your house down!" shouted the wolf. And he huffed and he puffed and he blew with all his might. But the house remained standing.

The wolf was *furious*. "If they won't let me in the door," he said to himself, "I'll climb down the chimney!"

But the third little pig heard the wolf creeping across the roof and he quickly put a huge pot of water on the fire. When the wolf jumped down the chimney, he landed with a splash in the pot and was boiled to bits. And that was the end of the big, bad wolf!

The Hare and the Tortoise

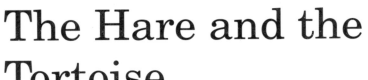

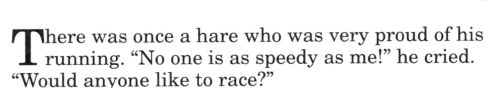

There was once a hare who was very proud of his running. "No one is as speedy as me!" he cried. "Would anyone like to race?"

"No thanks!" laughed the other animals. "We know you can run faster than any of us. We'd be silly to try to race you."

It was the same every day. The hare would boast about his running to everyone he met and no one dared to race him.

But one fine day, a little voice piped up politely behind him. "I'll give you a race if you like, Mr. Hare," it said.

The hare turned around in surprise. Standing before him was a wrinkly old tortoise, blinking in the sunshine. "Oh my!" replied the hare sarcastically. "You make me quake and tremble, *Mr.* Tortoise."

But the old tortoise was serious and the animals who had gathered around said, "You're always wanting to race, Hare. Let's see you do it!" So it was agreed that the hare and the tortoise would race to the old oak tree and back.

"On your marks! Get set! Go!" yelled the squirrel, waving her tail, and the runners set off.

In a couple of seconds the hare was nearly out of sight. The tortoise set off in his usual slow way. There seemed no doubt that the hare would win before the tortoise even reached the oak tree.

"Come on, Mr. Tortoise," the hare yelled over his shoulder. "This isn't much of a race!" But the tortoise saved his breath and kept plodding along.

When he reached the oak tree, the hare felt a little out of breath. For the past few months he had done more boasting than running. In any case, he knew that he was going to win easily, so he sat down under the oak tree to rest. It was a very hot day. The hare's eyelids began to close and soon he was fast asleep.

Now, all the time that the hare was dozing, the tortoise was ambling purposefully along. He took things steadily and never stopped for a rest.

An hour later, the hare woke up under the tree. He could hear cheering in the distance. Leaping to his feet, he set off as fast as his legs would carry him toward the finish line. He had never run so hard in his life. Surely he could catch the tortoise! But the tortoise's old head bobbed over the line a whisker before the hare's.

"Hurray for our new champion!" yelled all the animals.

I have heard that Mr. Hare hasn't been boasting so much lately. "Being quick on your feet is a fine thing, but slow and steady wins the race," said Mr. Tortoise.

The Fox and the Goat

One long, hot summer, a fox wandered slowly through the countryside, pleased to see how the sun made his red coat shine. He was so busy admiring himself that he didn't notice an old well in an abandoned garden. Before he knew what was happening, he had tumbled over the edge and into the well.

Now there was not very much water in the well, so the fox was quite safe at the bottom, but the well was deep and its sides were smooth and straight. The fox quickly realized that he could not climb out again.

For several long hours, the fox paddled around and around in the shallow water at the bottom of the well. He was afraid that he would never escape.

Suddenly, the fox's gloomy thoughts were interrupted by a foolish face peering over the top of the well.

"Hello down there!" boomed a voice. It was a goat, who had heard the splashing of the water and come to see what was happening.

The cunning fox at once saw his chance. "My friend," he called, "you have come just in time to share my good fortune. On such a hot day as this, have you ever seen anything as delightful as this cool water? I can tell you, it is quite delicious."

"But how can I reach it?" bleated the goat. "It is so far down."

"Why, jump, my friend!" cried the fox. "I promise you, you'll be quite safe. That's how I came down."

So the silly goat jumped into the well and found that the water was indeed cool and delicious. But before long, even the goat began to wonder how they could get out of the well again.

"Easy, my friend," said the fox. "Put your front feet as high up the wall as you can. I'll climb onto your back, balance on your horns, and jump to the top. Then I'll help you to get out."

Without thinking, the goat did as the fox suggested. In seconds, a grinning red face was looking down at him. "My poor friend," said the fox, "I'm afraid I can't stop to help you after all. I hope someone else comes along!" And the fox skipped off through the trees.

Like the well, the moral of this story is deep: Remember to look before you leap.

Puss in Boots

Once upon a time there was a miller who had three sons. The miller loved his sons very much, but he was not a rich man. When he died he left his mill to the eldest son and his donkey to the middle son. All he could leave the youngest son was the cat that caught mice at the mill.

"You are a fine mouser, Puss," said the youngest son sadly. "But I don't know how that is going to help me make a living."

"Don't worry, Master," said the cat. "Just give me a pair of your old boots and a bag and you'll find that we get along very well."

The miller's son was astonished but he did as Puss asked. The clever cat put some lettuce leaves in a bag and left it in a field. When a little rabbit came out and nibbled at the leaves, Puss jumped out from his hiding place and caught the rabbit in the bag. Then he set off for the King's palace.

The servants were amazed to see a cat wearing boots, so they led him to the King.

"Your Majesty," said Puss, bowing low, "I am your loyal servant and hope that you will accept this present of a fine, plump rabbit."

The King was very amused by the cat's fine ways. "Who is your master, Puss?" he asked.

"My master is the Marquis of Carrabas," said the cat grandly.

After that the cat very often visited the King. One day he learned that the King was going to take a drive along the river with his daughter, the Princess.

"Master," said Puss, "today you must go for a swim in the river and pretend that you have a new name. From now on, you are the Marquis of Carrabas."

Later that day, the King was driving along the riverbank in his carriage when he saw Puss running up and down in distress.

"Oh Your Majesty," cried Puss, "a terrible thing has happened. My master, the Marquis of Carrabas, was swimming in the river and some thieves stole his clothes!" (In fact, Puss had hidden them in some bushes nearby.)

In no time at all the King had sent for a fine suit of clothes to be brought for the young man. When he was dressed, he was invited to ride in the royal carriage and be introduced to the Princess.

Meanwhile Puss was running along the road ahead. When he saw some haymakers in a field, he said fiercely, "When the King comes by, if you don't say that this field belongs to the Marquis of Carrabas, you'll be minced into little bits and eaten!"

The workmen were so frightened that they did just as Puss said. In fact, every field the King passed seemed to belong to the Marquis. "I congratulate you on your fine lands, My Lord," said the King. The miller's son didn't know what to say, so he smiled at the Princess instead.

While this was happening, Puss had reached a huge castle. Bravely, he walked straight up to the ogre who owned it.

"I've heard you can do magic, Your Giantness," said Puss. "I should so love to see some."

The ogre gave a great roar of laughter and turned himself into a lion! Puss was very frightened but he pretended not to be.

"That's quite good," he said. "But I expect it would be more difficult for a great fellow like you to turn himself into something small like … er … a mouse?"

The ogre became a mouse in a second. But in less than a second Puss had pounced! The ogre made a very tasty snack indeed.

When the King arrived at the castle, everything was ready.

"Welcome to my master's home, Your Majesty," said Puss.

Of course, the King was very impressed and the Princess was even more impressed. Before long she and the miller's son were married and lived happily ever after in the castle.

And Puss? Well, the castle's cellars turned out to be absolutely full of mice. So Puss lived happily ever after as well.

Town Mouse and Country Mouse

Once upon a time there was a busy little mouse who lived in the country. One morning, as he was sweeping empty nutshells from his doorway, he saw a familiar figure coming down the road. It was his cousin, who lived in the town nearby.

"Hello cousin!" said Town Mouse. "I was getting tired of the hustle and bustle of town, so I thought I'd have a nice peaceful rest in the country."

"The pleasure is mine," said Country Mouse. "Welcome to my home." And he led his cousin into his snug little house in the roots of an ancient oak tree.

But that night, Country Mouse was awakened by a forlorn little figure standing by his bed.

"Oh cousin," said Town Mouse. "I'm so frightened. I couldn't get to sleep because your straw mattress tickled me so. And then I heard horrible rustling and scurrying noises outside."

Country Mouse listened. "Those are just ordinary country sounds," he said. "You'll find that you soon get used to them."

The next day, Country Mouse got busy as usual, picking berries and seeds to store for the winter. "Come and help me!" he said to his cousin. But Town Mouse didn't like hard work or getting his hands dirty. "We have plenty of food in town, without having to work for it," he said.

Country Mouse wanted to be kind. "I'll finish my work and make us a picnic," he said. "You'll like that."

But the picnic was not a great success. Town Mouse was frightened of the big cows and horses. On the way home, Country Mouse pulled his cousin quickly into a hedge as an owl flew by. Town Mouse made up his mind. "I'm going home," he said, "and you must come too, cousin. You'll love life in town. There is no work to do and we sleep on real feather beds and eat delicious food. You'll never want to come home."

So Country Mouse set off with Town Mouse. After a
long day's journey they reached the town and came to
the big house where Town Mouse lived.

"Isn't it splendid?" yelled Town Mouse. But Country
Mouse could hardly hear him because of the traffic.

Inside, the house was large and luxurious. "I'm
afraid of getting lost," said Country Mouse nervously.

The mice had all the food they could eat from the
pantry. But Country Mouse found it too rich and
sweet. "I think I'll go to bed now," he said. "I don't feel
very well."

Tucked up between soft sheets on a feather
mattress, Country Mouse was very comfortable – but
he didn't get a wink of sleep! The streetlights and the
noise of the traffic kept him awake all night.

The next morning, Town Mouse whisked Country Mouse out of the way just as a large cat was about to catch him for his breakfast! It was the last straw.

"Thank you so much for having me to stay," said Country Mouse, "but I'm going straight home!"

It was a very tired little mouse who arrived back at the old oak tree that evening, but Country Mouse snuggled down on his old straw mattress with a big smile on his face. "Visiting is all very nice," he said, "but there's no place like home!"

Old MacDonald

Old MacDonald had a farm,
EE-I-EE-I-O!
And on that farm he had some hens,
EE-I-EE-I-O!
With a cluck, cluck here,
And a cluck, cluck there!
Here a cluck, there a cluck,
Everywhere a cluck, cluck!
Old MacDonald had a farm,
EE-I-EE-I-O!

Old MacDonald had a farm,
EE-I-EE-I-O!
And on that farm he had some sheep,
EE-I-EE-I-O!
With a baa, baa here…

Old MacDonald had a farm,
EE-I-EE-I-O!
And on that farm he had some pigs,
EE-I-EE-I-O!
With an oink, oink here…

Old MacDonald had a farm,
EE-I-EE-I-O!
And on that farm he had some ducks,
EE-I-EE-I-O!
With a quack, quack here…

Old MacDonald had a farm,
EE-I-EE-I-O!
And on that farm he had some cows,
EE-I-EE-I-O!
With a moo, moo here…

Old MacDonald had a farm,
EE-I-EE-I-O!
And on that farm he had some geese,
EE-I-EE-I-O!
With a honk, honk here…

Old MacDonald had a farm,
EE-I-EE-I-O!
And on that farm he had a dog,
EE-I-EE-I-O!
With a woof, woof here…

Old MacDonald had a farm,
EE-I-EE-I-O!
And on that farm he had a cat,
EE-I-EE-I-O!
With a meow, meow here…

Old MacDonald had a farm,
EE-I-EE-I-O!
And on that farm he had a tractor,
EE-I-EE-I-O!
With a brrrm, brrrm here,
And a brrrm, brrrm there!
Here a brrrm, there a brrrm,
Everywhere a brrrm, brrrm!
Old MacDonald had a farm,
EE-I-EE-I-O!

The Ant and the Grasshopper

Long ago on a sunny hillside, there lived an ant and a grasshopper. The grasshopper was a handsome insect with a glossy green coat. All day long he sat in the sun and made music, filling the hillside with his summery sounds.

The ant was a very different character. Small and dark, she bustled about every day, collecting grass seeds to store in her nest. From morning to night she was never still.

"Why are you so silly, Ant?" asked the grasshopper lazily. "The sun is shining but you never stop to smell the flowers or look up at the sky. Life is too short to be always scurrying and hurrying."

But the ant could not be persuaded to slow down. "Summer will not last forever, Grasshopper," she said. "I must get ready for the cold winter that is coming."

"Ho ho," laughed the grasshopper. "I don't believe that winter will ever come!" and his music rang out over the hillside once more.

But soon the leaves began to fall from the trees. The flowers died and clouds floated across the sky. It grew colder and colder. At last one day, feathery flakes of snow began to fall across the hillside.

The ant was snug in her nest under a stone. She had enough food for the winter. Outside she heard a faint chirruping sound. It was the grasshopper.

"Dear Ant," he croaked. "Please give me some food. I haven't any at all stored up for myself."

But the Ant was firm. "I'm sorry, Grasshopper," she said. "But you should have thought of that before. If I give you food, I won't have enough to feed my family."

A thick layer of snow settled over the hillside. All was still and quiet, and the music of the grasshopper was heard no more.

The Little Red Hen

Once there was a little red hen who found some grains of wheat. She carried them off to the farmyard and asked the other animals, "Who will help me to plant this wheat?"

But the cat said, "Not I!"

And the rat said, "Not I!"

And the pig said, "Not I!"

"Then I shall plant it myself," said the little red hen. And so she did.

The days passed and the wheat began to grow. By the end of the summer it was high and golden. The little red hen went to the farmyard again and asked, "Who will help me harvest my wheat?"

But the cat said, "Not I!"

And the rat said, "Not I!"

And the pig said, "Not I!"

"Then I shall harvest it myself," said the little red hen. And so she did.

It took the little red hen many days to cut down all the wheat and shake the grains into a big sack. When she had finished, she went back to the farmyard and asked, "Who will help me take my wheat to the miller to make it into flour?"

But the cat said, "Not I!"

And the rat said, "Not I!"

And the pig said, "Not I!"

"Then I shall take it to the mill myself," said the little red hen.

She dragged the big sack slowly to the mill and the miller ground the grain into flour.

The little red hen took her flour back to the farmyard and asked, "Who will help me take my flour to the baker to be made into bread?"

But the cat said, "Not I!"

And the rat said, "Not I!"

And the pig said, "Not I!"

"Then I shall take it to the baker myself," said the little red hen.

She went to the baker and he made four beautiful brown loaves with the flour.

The little red hen took the loaves back to the farmyard and asked, "Who would like to help me to eat my delicious bread?"

"I would!" said the cat.

And "I would!" said the rat.

And "I would!" said the pig.

"Then I shall eat it all myself," said the little red hen. And so she did.

The Elephant and the Mouse

Long ago and far away
Lived an elephant, huge and gray.
As he walked beside the brook,
All of the jungle shivered and shook.

One day the elephant chanced to be
Strolling beneath a banana tree.
From his feet on the sandy ground,
His ears caught a tiny crying sound.

"Oh please be careful!" he heard it wail,
"You're standing heavily on my tail!"
The elephant looked down in surprise
To see what was making the piercing cries.

Between the elephant's big gray toes,
A little mouse was twitching his nose.
"Please lift your foot and let me free!
And you'll be glad one day, you'll see!"

Said the elephant, "Please don't be alarmed.
A fellow creature should not be harmed."
He raised his foot and the mouse ran away,
Not to be seen for many a long day.

As the months passed by in the jungle heat,
The elephant gently placed his feet.
He kept his eyes upon the ground
And didn't see the hunters gather around!

When he raised his head, it was far too late.
He was caught in a net, awaiting his fate.
Then a tiny voice whispered in his ear,
"Don't worry, Elephant, you've nothing to fear!"

There was the mouse from months before!
He bit into the net and began to gnaw.
In the blink of an eye, the elephant was free.
"Thank you," he said, "for rescuing me."

The moral of this story is plain to view,
If you help others, then they'll help you!

The Wolf and the Seven Little Kids

Once upon a time there was a mother goat who had seven little kids. One day the mother goat had to go into the forest to find some food but before she went she spoke seriously to her seven children.

"My dears," she said. "While I am gone you must keep the door shut and not open it to anyone. Above all you must never open it to Mr. Wolf, because he would like to eat you for his supper. You can always tell when Mr. Wolf comes calling, no matter how he disguises himself, because he has a gruff voice and rough hairy paws."

The little kids promised that they would be very careful, and their mother set off for the forest. But before very long there came a knock at the door.

"My dears," said a gruff voice, "it's your mother home from the forest. Let me in!"

"You are not our mother," said the kids. "She doesn't have a gruff voice like you. Go away!"

At this Mr. Wolf, for of course that was who it was, ran quickly home. He drank a special honey drink that his granny used to make and his voice became soft and sweet. Then he hurried back to the kids' little cottage.

"My dears," he said, in his soft voice, "it's your mother home from the forest. Let me in!" But as he spoke, he laid one of his paws on the window sill and one of the little kids saw it. "You are not our mother," he cried. "She doesn't have rough hairy paws. Go away!"

At this Mr. Wolf was very angry. He ran off to the baker's shop and dipped his paws into the dough. Now he had smooth white paws, not rough hairy ones. Then he hurried back to the cottage and knocked on the door.

"My dears," he called, "it's your mother home from the forest. Let me in!" The little kids heard his soft voice and saw his smooth white feet on the window sill. "It *is* mother!" they cried and they opened the door.

At once Mr. Wolf came bounding in. In the blink of an eye he had gobbled up all the little kids except the smallest one of all, who hid inside the clock. After his meal, Mr. Wolf was very sleepy. He lay down under a tree and was soon snoring away.

Meanwhile, the mother goat had come home. "Where are my babies?" she cried, as she saw the open front door. At last the very smallest kid crept out of the clock and told her what had happened.

"Just wait until I find that wolf!" said the mother goat. Mr. Wolf wasn't hard to find because he was snoring so loudly. The mother goat looked closely at his fat tummy. She could see something moving inside! Snip! Snip! With her sewing scissors she made a little hole and out jumped the six little kids! The wolf had been so greedy that he had swallowed them whole.

As Mr. Wolf slept on, the seven little kids each brought a big stone and popped it into the hole that their mother had made. Then she sewed up Mr. Wolf's tummy and they all tiptoed away.

When Mr. Wolf woke up, he felt quite odd and very thirsty. At once he staggered off to the well nearby.

"I thought I had swallowed six little kids," he said. "But they feel more like six big rocks in my tummy!" When Mr. Wolf got to the well, the stones in his tummy were so heavy that he toppled over and fell right into the water.

Bad Mr. Wolf was never seen again and the mother goat and her seven little kids lived happily ever after.

The Ugly Duckling

There was once a mother duck who lived on a pond near a farm. All spring she sat on her nest by the bank, keeping her five big eggs warm under her feathers.

"Haven't those eggs hatched yet?" clucked a hen, as she led her fluffy chickens past the pond.

"It won't be long now," replied the mother duck sharply. "And they will be very beautiful, swimming birds when they do hatch."

Sure enough, a few days later, a faint tapping sound could be heard. One, two, three, four little fluffy ducklings hatched from the eggs. Last of all, with a squawk and a wriggle, the largest egg hatched.

The mother duck looked carefully at her fifth little duckling. He was a fine strong bird, much bigger than all the other ducklings, but there was no doubt about it: he was ugly.

"Very pretty, my dear," said the other ducks, when the mother duck took her new ducklings for their first swim. "Except for that one. *What* an ugly duckling!"

"He's just big for his age," said the mother duck. "He'll grow into his looks, you'll see."

But every day that went by, the strange duckling looked less and less like a neat little farm duck. The other ducks jeered at him and pecked him when his mother wasn't looking. The duckling was so unhappy that one day he ran away.

"I shall go and live with the wild ducks," he said to himself. "They won't be unkind to me."

The ugly duckling wandered until he came to the great marsh where the wild ducks lived. He saw them flying overhead and began to feel better. But the wild ducks took one look at him and began to laugh.

"Go away!" they quacked. "You'll frighten our ducklings."

So the ugly duckling ran away again. He walked wearily over fields and through woods. At last, as night was falling, he came to a cottage. He settled down on the doorstep out of the cold wind and went to sleep.

In the morning, the old woman who lived in the cottage found the sleeping duckling. "You can stay," she said kindly, "with my hen and my cat."

But the hen clucked disapprovingly. "Can you lay eggs?" she asked.

"No," said the ugly duckling.

"Can you purr?" asked the cat.

"Oh no," squawked the duckling.

"Then you are no use here at all," said the cat and the hen, and they chased the duckling away.

For many months the ugly duckling wandered the marshes and meadows. One afternoon in late autumn, the duckling saw some beautiful white birds flying overhead.

"If only I looked like that," he said.

The weather grew colder. One morning the duckling awoke to find the marsh had frozen and he was stuck in the ice.

Luckily a kind farmer rescued him and took him home. The farmer's wife gave him food and for a few days the duckling was happy. But the farmer's children chased him and wanted to play with him. The duckling grew frightened. One day he ran away again.

All winter long, the duckling lived among the reeds of the marsh. He could fly now on his long, strong wings. As he flew, he looked down at the water and saw three of the beautiful white birds below. They were swans.

"If only I could live near them, I would be happy," thought the duckling, and he flew down and landed on the clear water. As he did so, he caught sight of his own reflection and could hardly believe what he saw. He wasn't an ugly duckling at all! He was a beautiful swan, with an elegant long neck and pure white feathers.

As he landed, the other swans swam over and greeted him as though he were a long lost friend. Proudly, the young swan swam among them. He was home at last.

The Owl and the Pussy Cat

The Owl and the Pussy Cat went to sea
In a beautiful pea green boat:
They took some honey, and plenty of money
Wrapped up in a five pound note.
The Owl looked up to the stars above,
And sang to a small guitar,
"O lovely Pussy, O Pussy, my love,
What a beautiful Pussy you are,
     You are,
     You are!
What a beautiful Pussy you are!"

Pussy said to the Owl, "You elegant fowl,
How charmingly sweet you sing!
Oh! Let us be married; too long we have tarried:
But what shall we do for a ring?"
They sailed away, for a year and a day,
To the land where the bong-tree grows;
And there in a wood a Piggy-wig stood,
With a ring at the end of his nose,
     His nose,
     His nose,
With a ring at the end of his nose.

"Dear Pig, are you willing to sell for one shilling
Your ring?" Said the Piggy, "I will."
So they took it away, and were married next day
By the turkey who lives on the hill.
They dined on mince and slices of quince,
Which they ate with a runcible spoon;
And hand in hand, on the edge of the sand,
They danced by the light of the moon,
    The moon,
    The moon,
They danced by the light of the moon.

Androcles and the Lion

Long ago there lived a young man called Androcles. He was not a free man, for he was owned as a slave by a rich Roman merchant who lived in Africa. This man treated his slaves very badly. Androcles was forced to work from dawn until dusk. He had hardly any food and was often beaten cruelly. One morning, when he saw his master coming to beat him again, Androcles could bear it no longer. With the furious shouts of the merchant ringing in his ears, he ran from the house and out into the countryside.

By midday, Androcles was too tired to run any further. The African sun beat down without mercy. He looked desperately for somewhere shady to hide and caught sight of the opening to a cave. Weak with hunger and exhaustion, Androcles crawled inside.

For a few minutes, the runaway slave rested against the cool rock wall. Suddenly, a fearsome roar echoed through the cave and a huge shape leaped toward him. It was a lion! Terrified, Androcles closed his eyes. But no attack came. Instead the slave heard a soft whimpering noise, like a lost kitten.

Androcles opened his eyes and looked at the lion. It was holding one paw off the ground. Androcles could see a large thorn buried deep in the paw, which looked sore and swollen. He hated to see a fellow creature in pain. Speaking soothingly to the huge animal, he gently pulled out the thorn.

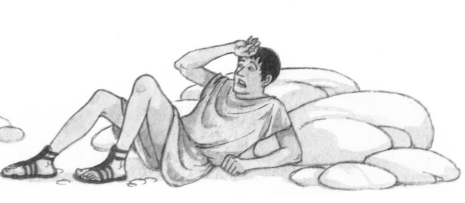

The lion put its foot back on the ground and felt at once that the pain was much less. With a grunt, it turned and padded softly out of the cave.

For several days, Androcles hid in the cave, but he had to go out to find food and water. On one of these trips, he was spotted by some of the merchant's men and captured. He was dragged to the dungeons underneath the arena. This was a huge building where fights and shows were staged. Androcles knew what awaited him – to be torn apart by wild animals in front of thousands of people.

On the morning of the spectacle, two soldiers dragged Androcles from his cell and pushed him into the arena. On seats high above, Androcles could see row upon row of faces. Then the doors of the animals' cage opened and a fierce lion leaped out, roaring at the top of its voice. Androcles fell to his knees, believing that his last moments had come.

The next moment he felt a rough tongue licking his face and looked up to see the lion that he had helped standing before him. Instead of attacking him, the lion rubbed its head against him, just like a pet cat does.

"So you are a prisoner, too, old friend," whispered Androcles, stroking the shaggy mane.

The crowd loved this extraordinary display even more than seeing the lion tear the slave apart. They cheered and clapped, until the Roman Governor, trying to make himself more popular, announced that Androcles should be released.

And so the slave's kindness was rewarded and he walked away from the arena a free man at last.

The Nightingale

Long ago in China, there lived a great Emperor. He was richer and more powerful than any Emperor who had ever lived. His palace was as big as a city and beautifully decorated with porcelain and silver and gold. Around the palace there was a garden that stretched further than the eye could see. It was full of the loveliest plants and trees. Little streams sparkled in the sun and deep pools reflected the delicate flowers that grew along their banks. Everyone agreed that it was the most beautiful garden in the world.

Among the trees of the Emperor's garden, there lived a little brown bird who was not very beautiful at all. It was a nightingale. When the nightingale opened her mouth and sang, the notes came trickling out like pearls from a silken purse. Everyone who heard it forgot their troubles. They even forgot the beautiful garden and the powerful Emperor. They all said that the nightingale's song was the loveliest thing they had ever heard.

One day the Emperor himself was told of the nightingale's song. "Why have I never heard this remarkable bird?" he asked. "Bring her to me at once!"

The Emperor's Chief Minister ran to the garden and explained to the nightingale that the rich and powerful Emperor wished to hear her sing.

"Gladly," said the nightingale. "Take me to the palace."

That evening, when the whole court was assembled in the throne room, the nightingale sang for the Emperor. Everyone who heard her wept at the lovely sound. As for the Emperor, the tears ran from his eyes like diamonds.

"Put the bird in a golden cage," he cried. "I must hear this heavenly music every day."

The poor nightingale hated to be imprisoned in a cage. She grew more and more unhappy. At last she was so sad that she could not sing at all. The Emperor was furious. He ordered his wisest men to make a mechanical nightingale that would sing whenever it was wound up.

The wisest men in the kingdom worked for a year on the mechanical bird. When they had finished they brought it before the Emperor. "This bird is even better than the real nightingale, Great Emperor," they said.

The mechanical bird was covered with gold. Precious jewels sparkled on its back and wings. When its golden key was turned, a beautiful song came from its beak. Everyone agreed that it was even better than the real nightingale. It was much more beautiful to look at and its song never changed. The real nightingale was allowed to fly out into the garden.

For five years the mechanical bird sang to the Emperor every day. But its mechanisms became worn with use and perhaps its song was not quite so beautiful as once it had been.

Then one day, the Emperor fell ill. For weeks he lay in his state chambers, growing weaker and weaker. Everyone believed that the Emperor was going to die. More and more they left the sick man alone, while they went to pay court to the Prince who would become the new Emperor. One evening, the Emperor felt that death was very near.

Alone in his room, he longed one last time to hear the notes of the nightingale. But he was too weak to turn the golden key.

Then, from the open window, the lovely song floated into the room. The real nightingale sat on a branch outside, singing as though her heart would break.

"Sleep, my Emperor, and become strong again," she sang. "You know now that beauty cannot be caged and gifts must be freely given."

So the Emperor slept. In the morning, when the courtiers came, expecting to find that he had died in the night, the Emperor was better than he had been for months. Every night, the nightingale sang soothingly to him, telling him things that were valuable and true. Soon the Emperor was completely well but he was a changed man. He ruled for many more years and the people, who had once feared him, now loved him for his kindness and wisdom.

Peter and the Wolf

Once there was a little boy who lived with his grandfather. Every day he went into the big garden behind the house and played with the birds and the animals who visited him there. But his grandfather said, "Peter, you must never, ever go out of the garden and into the meadow. For the wolf may come out of the forest and eat you!"

Peter promised that he would stay in the garden, but secretly he thought that his grandfather was worrying about nothing. One sunny morning, he opened the garden gate and walked out into the big green meadow.

High in a tree, a little bird was singing. "Hello, Peter," she sang. "What are doing all alone in the meadow?"

"Just walking," said Peter. "You haven't seen the wolf today, have you?"

"Oh no, not today," said the bird. "When the wolf is hungry, no one is safe. Look at that duck. She has followed you from the garden. You must warn her about the wolf."

But the duck wanted to swim in the pond in the meadow. "Come and join me," she shouted to the bird. "It's lovely in here!"

"No, no, no," chirruped the bird. "Swimming's no good. Flying is much better." And she fluttered up and down on the bank to show how well she could fly.

But the bird didn't see that a cat was creeping through the grass behind her.

"I'll have that bird for my dinner," thought the cat. "She's too busy showing off to the duck to notice me."

Luckily, Peter turned around just at that minute. "Look out!" he called to the bird. As the cat sprang, the bird flew safely up into a tree. "Thank you, Peter," she sang.

A little later, Peter's grandfather came out into the garden. He saw that the gate was open and heard the singing and quacking and laughing coming from the meadow.

"Peter!" he shouted. "Come back into the garden at once!" Again, Peter promised not to leave the garden.

Meanwhile, out in the meadow, a gray, shadowy shape crept out of the forest. The cat leaped up into the tree. The bird flew up and landed beside the cat. But the duck was too slow as she flapped across the grass. In a flash, the wolf had swallowed her whole. Then he prowled up and down under the tree. The cat and the bird huddled together on the branch.

Peter had seen what had happened from the garden. All at once he thought of a clever plan to save the cat and the bird. "I will not be afraid of that old wolf," he said to himself.

Peter fetched a piece of rope and climbed up onto the garden wall. "Fly around the wolf's head and make him dizzy," he called to the bird. Distracted by the bird, the wolf did not see Peter tie one end of the rope to the tree and make a loop in the other end.

Then he dangled the rope down and caught the wolf by the tail! The harder the wolf pulled, the tighter the rope became. Now the wolf was feeling very sick indeed. The bird had made him dizzy and he had a very strange feeling in his tummy.

Just then some hunters came out of the forest. "Over here!" cried Peter. "We have caught the wolf!" Peter's grandfather came out to see what the noise was.

"I haven't gone out of the garden, grandfather," laughed Peter, from the top of the wall.

There was a grand procession as the hunters took the wolf to the zoo. Peter led the wolf at the end of the rope. He was happy that the wolf would be looked after and not eat the other animals any more. The bird flew overhead and the cat prowled along behind. Even the wolf was happy. He hoped that the keepers at the zoo would make the strange feeling in his tummy better.

"Quack! Quack!" Inside the wolf the duck was feeling happier too. She stamped her feet with joy to think that she would soon be rescued. No wonder the poor wolf wasn't feeling very well!

Noah's Ark

Long ago there was a very good man called Noah. He always tried to do what was right, even if it meant that his friends laughed at him.

One day, God spoke to Noah. "Everywhere wicked people are spoiling the world and not living as they should," He said. "Only you and your family are trying to follow my laws, Noah. I am going to wash away all the wickedness in the world, but you will be saved. I want you to build a huge boat, an ark, and put on it your wife and family and two of every kind of animal on earth."

Noah was astonished. "We live miles from the sea," he thought. "I've never built a boat in my life."

But God gave Noah instructions explaining how to build the boat, and the good man set to work.

"Going away?" jeered people passing. "You won't get very far in that!"

But Noah worked steadily on.

"Oh, you're building a cabin on it now," laughed the foolish people a few weeks later. "It's a round-the-world trip, is it?"

"Well, I think it might be," said Noah thoughtfully. "You're welcome to join me if you like." But the people roared with laughter and went home.

When the ark was finished, Noah called his sons and their wives to him and asked them to help him round up two of every kind of animal on earth.

"*Every* kind?" asked his youngest son, who didn't like spiders very much.

"*Every* kind," said Noah firmly. "And we'll need to be careful that they don't eat each other."

So two by two, the animals were led to their places in the ark. The elephants nearly broke the gangplank and the monkeys kept escaping, but at last they were all safely on board. Then Noah and his family took their places and God shut the great doors of the ark.

People from near and far came round to laugh and joke. "Aren't you forgetting just one thing?" they asked. "What about some water to float on?"

Almost at once, black clouds rolled across the sky and heavy rain began to fall. Once it started, it just didn't stop. Day after day it fell in a steady stream.

The ark gave a lurch and a roll. "We're floating!" cried Noah. "Batten down the hatches!"

For forty days and nights the ark floated on the floods. The water covered the houses and the hills. Everywhere you looked, there was only water. Huge whales and little fish swam beside the ark.

At last the rain stopped. "Soon the floods will begin to go down," said Noah. "We must find dry land."

"The sooner, the better," said his wife. For the ark was becoming just a bit smelly.

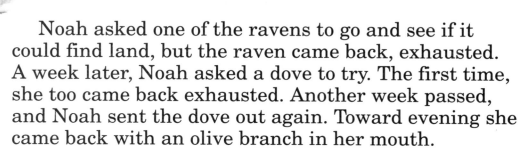

Noah asked one of the ravens to go and see if it could find land, but the raven came back, exhausted. A week later, Noah asked a dove to try. The first time, she too came back exhausted. Another week passed, and Noah sent the dove out again. Toward evening she came back with an olive branch in her mouth.

"The water must be going down," cried Noah. After another week, he sent the dove out for a third time. This time she did not return. "She has found a place to build a nest," said Noah. The next day, with a bump and a jolt, the ark settled on the top of a mountain.

Joyfully, Noah and his family climbed out of the ark, and the animals followed them. There were more of them than at the beginning. Noah lifted his hands to heaven and thanked God for saving their lives.

"You have done well, Noah," said God. "I promise that I will never again destroy the world that I have made."

And God made a rainbow to arch from the earth to the heavens and remind us all of His promise.

Chicken Licken

One day as Chicken Licken was walking along, an acorn fell on his head. "Oh my goodness," said Chicken Licken. "The sky is falling in! I must go at once and tell the King."

So Chicken Licken set off to find the King. On the way he met Henny Penny. "Where are you going, Chicken Licken?" she asked.

"The sky is falling in," said Chicken Licken, "and I am going to tell the King."

"Then I shall come too," said Henny Penny.

So Chicken Licken and Henny Penny set off to find the King. On the way they met Cocky Locky. "Where are you going to, Chicken Licken and Henny Penny?" he asked.

"The sky is falling in," cried Chicken Licken, "and we are going to tell the King."

"Then I shall come too," said Cocky Locky.

So Chicken Licken and Henny Penny and Cocky Locky set off to find the King.

On the way they met Ducky Lucky. "Where are you off to, Chicken Licken, Henny Penny and Cocky Locky?" she asked.

"The sky is falling in," cried Chicken Licken, "and we are going to tell the King."

"Then I shall come too," said Ducky Lucky.

So Chicken Licken and Henny Penny and Cocky Locky and Ducky Lucky set off to find the King. On the way they met Drakey Lakey. "Where are you hurrying to, Chicken Licken, Henny Penny, Cocky Locky and Ducky Lucky?" he asked.

"The sky is falling in," cried Chicken Licken, "and we are going to tell the King."

"Then I shall come too," said Drakey Lakey.

So Chicken Licken, Henny Penny, Cocky Locky, Ducky Lucky and Drakey Lakey set off to find the King. On the way they met Goosey Loosey. "Where are you going so quickly, Chicken Licken, Henny Penny, Cocky Locky, Ducky Lucky and Drakey Lakey?" asked Goosey Loosey.

"The sky is falling in," cried Chicken Licken, "and we are going to tell the King."

"Then I shall come too," said Drakey Lakey.

So Chicken Licken, Henny Penny, Cocky Locky, Ducky Lucky, Drakey Lakey and Goosey Loosey set off to find the King.

On the way they met Turkey Lurkey. "Where are you going, Chicken Licken, Henny Penny, Cocky Locky, Ducky Lucky, Drakey Lakey and Goosey Loosey?" he asked.

"The sky is falling in," cried Chicken Licken, "and we are going to tell the King."

"Then I shall come too," said Turkey Lurkey.

So Chicken Licken, Henny Penny, Cocky Locky, Ducky Lucky, Drakey Lakey, Goosey Loosey and Turkey Lurkey set off to find the King. On the way they met Foxy Loxy. "Where are you off to this fine morning, my dears?" he asked.

"The sky is falling in," cried Chicken Licken. "We are going to tell the King."

"Then follow me," said Foxy Loxy. "For I know the way very well."

So Chicken Licken, Henny Penny, Cocky Locky, Ducky Lucky, Drakey Lakey, Goosey Loosey and Turkey Lurkey followed Foxy Loxy. But he didn't lead them to the King. Instead he took them to his den in the forest and there Foxy Loxy and his wife and all his children ate Chicken Licken, Henny Penny, Cocky Locky, Ducky Lucky, Drakey Lakey, Goosey Loosey and Turkey Lurkey for their breakfast!

So Chicken Licken, Henny Penny, Cocky Locky, Ducky Lucky, Drakey Lakey, Goosey Loosey and Turkey Lurkey never did get to see the King. But then the sky didn't fall in either!

Who Killed Cock Robin?

Who killed Cock Robin?
I, said the Sparrow,
With my bow and arrow,
I killed Cock Robin.

Who saw him die?
I, said the Fly,
With my little eye,
I saw him die.

Who caught his blood?
I, said the Fish,
With my little dish,
I caught his blood.

Who'll make the shroud?
I, said the Beetle,
With my thread and needle,
I'll make the shroud.

Who'll dig the grave?
I, said the Owl,
With my pick and shovel,
I'll dig his grave.

Who'll be the parson?
I, said the Rook,
With my little book,
I'll be the parson.

Who'll be the clerk?
I, said the Lark,
If it's not in the dark,
I'll be the clerk.

All the birds of the air
Fell a-sighing and a-sobbing,
When they heard the bell toll
For poor Cock Robin.

A Present for Percy

It's easy to buy a good present
For someone who's active and fun.
You find what they need for their hobbies
And buy the most suitable one.

But what do you buy for a piglet
Who spends all the time in his chair?
He only gets up when he's hungry,
And even that's getting quite rare.

You can't buy him socks or a sweater,
It really can make you depressed,
He just watches his big television
And most days he doesn't get dressed!

One Christmas his cousin Belinda
Gave Percy an exercise tape.
"Just ten minutes a day," she said, "Percy,
You'll soon be in wonderful shape!"

A month or two later Belinda
Asked, "Are you doing the tape as you should?"
Said Percy, "I find that I don't have to move,
Just watching it through does me good!"

So we've all given up on young Percy,
For buying him gifts is no fun.
Perhaps he'll do something dynamic,
When this year he doesn't get one!

To
Santa

The Three Billy Goats Gruff

Once there were three billy goats called Gruff. They lived in the mountains, scrambling over rocks and streams in search of the fresh, green grass they loved to eat.

One day the three billy goats Gruff stood on a hillside and looked down into the next valley. "That is the greenest grass I have seen for many a day," said the biggest billy goat, "but how can we reach it?" Between the billy goats and the fresh, green grass a wide river rushed along. It was far too wide and fast-flowing for the billy goats to swim across.

"We will walk along the bank," said the middle-sized billy goat, "until we come to a place where we can cross safely."

So the billy goats walked along the riverbank until they came to a narrow wooden bridge.

"No one seems to use the bridge, perhaps it is not very strong," said the smallest billy goat. "I am the lightest, so I will go first to make sure."

In fact the bridge was strong and safe but a wicked old troll lived underneath it. Whenever he heard footsteps on the bridge, he jumped out and ate anyone who tried to cross.

The smallest billy goat Gruff did not know this. *Trip, trap, trip, trap,* went his hooves on the wooden planks. Suddenly the ugly old troll's face popped over the edge of the bridge. "Who's that trip-trapping across *my* bridge?" he roared.

The little goat was almost too frightened to speak, but at last he said, "I'm the smallest billy goat Gruff."

"Well, I'm a troll," came the reply. "And I'm going to eat you for my dinner."

"Oh don't do that," said the smallest billy goat Gruff. "My brother is following me and he is much fatter than I am. He will make you a much better dinner than me."

The troll thought for a minute. The little goat looked very tasty, but a bigger goat would be better still. So he let the smallest billy goat Gruff go trip-trapping on across the bridge and onto the fresh, green grass on the other side.

When the middle-sized goat saw his brother jumping and running on the other side of the bridge, he decided to cross himself. *Trip, trap, trip, trap*, went his hooves on the wooden planks. In the very middle of the bridge, the ugly old troll popped up again. "Who's that trip-trapping across *my* bridge?" he roared.

The middle-sized billy goat Gruff was very frightened, too. He knew how much trolls love to eat fat mountain goats. But he answered bravely. "Oh, I'm the middle-sized billy goat Gruff," he said. "But you don't want to trouble yourself with me. My elder brother is following me and he will make a much better meal for a big, strong troll like you."

The greedy troll thought for a minute. Then he let the middle-sized goat go trip-trapping over the bridge, to run in the fresh, green grass on the other side.

Now the biggest billy goat Gruff had seen everything that had happened and he smiled to himself. His big hooves went *trip, trap, trip, trap,* on the wooden planks. It wasn't long before the troll jumped right out of his hiding place and stood in the middle of the bridge.

"Who's that trip-trapping across *my* bridge?" he roared, louder than ever.

"I'm the biggest billy goat Gruff," came the reply. "Move out of my way."

"Oh no," said the troll with an ugly sneer. "I've been waiting all morning for this. I'm going to eat you for my dinner!"

But the biggest billy goat Gruff set off down the bridge at a run. *TRIP, TRAP, TRIP, TRAP,* went his mighty hooves. When he reached the middle of the bridge, he lowered his horns and CHARGED!

With a great roar, the ugly old troll flew high up into the air. Then he fell with a huge splash into the river below. The fast-flowing water carried him far away, never to be seen again.

And the three billy goats Gruff found all the fresh, green grass they could wish for in the valley and lived happily ever after.

The Sly Fox and the
Little Red Hen

Once there was a little red hen who lived by herself in the woods. She had a neat little house, which she kept very clean. Her home kept her warm in the winter and safe at night from the sly fox who lived nearby with his mother.

One morning the little red hen went into the woods to collect some sticks for her fire. She worked hard and pretty soon she had a large bundle to carry home. But she didn't know that the sly young fox had been watching her all the while. When he saw that the little red hen was ready to go home, he ran quickly ahead and slipped into her neat little house. In a flash he had hidden himself behind the little red hen's strong front door.

The little red hen hurried up the steps to her house and carried her sticks inside. But the moment she shut the door, the sly young fox jumped out at her. Squawking with terror, the little red hen flew up to the roof and perched on one of the rafters. She thought that she would be safe there.

The sly young fox laughed to himself. "You can't escape from me so easily, Little Red Hen!" he said. And he began to act in a very strange manner.

"What ever is he *doing*?" said the little red hen to herself, as the fox chased his own tail around and around the room. She watched and watched until she became so dizzy that she dropped right off her perch.

Of course, that was just what the sly young fox had planned. He picked up the little red hen and popped her into a sack he had brought with him. "You will make a very fine dinner for my mother and me," he said, as he tied up the sack and set off back to his den in the woods.

The little red hen kept very quiet in the sack. She was thinking hard and wondering if she would have a chance to escape.

Pretty soon the fox became tired after all his watching and waiting and chasing.

He lay down near some rocks and went to sleep. When she heard him snoring, the little red hen pecked at the bag and made a hole near the top, just big enough for her to escape. Then she quietly gathered some large stones and put them into the sack. At last she tiptoed away and ran all the way back to her snug little home.

When the sly young fox woke up, he set off once more. "The little red hen feels even heavier than before," he said to himself. "I hope that my mother has a big pot of water boiling on the stove to cook this tasty little bird."

When he reached his den, the fox's mother was delighted. "The water is boiling, my clever boy," she said. "Throw her in at once."

The fox and his mother leaned over the pot as he undid the sack and tipped it upside down. With an enormous splash, the stones fell into the boiling water. The water splashed all over the two foxes and gave them the fright of their lives. They limped away from the woods and were never seen again.

The little red hen lived happily ever after. And after that, she always locked her door when she went out!